EDGE BOOKS™

CROSS-SECTIONS

THE AV-8B HARRIER JUMP JET

by Ole Steen Hansen
illustrated by Alex Pang
Consultant: Craig Hoyle, Defense Editor, Flight International

Capstone
press

Mankato, Minnesota

First published in the United States in 2006 by Capstone Press
151 Good Counsel Drive, P.O. Box 669, Mankato, Minnesota 56002
http://www.capstonepress.com

Library of Congress Cataloging-in-Publication Data
Hansen, Ole Steen.
    The AV-8B Harrier jump jet / by Ole Steen Hansen ; illustrated by Alex Pang.
    p. cm.—(Edge books, cross-sections)
    Summary: "An in-depth look at the AV-8B Harrier Jump Jet, with detailed cross-
section diagrams, action photos, and fascinating facts"—Provided by publisher.
    Includes bibliographical references and index.
    ISBN 0-7368-5254-9 (hardcover)
    1. Harrier (Jet fighter plane)—Juvenile literature. I. Pang, Alex, ill. II. Title. III.
Series.
UG1242.F5H356 2006
623.74'64—dc22   2005009642

Designed and produced by

David West ☖ Children's Books
7 Princeton Court
55 Felsham Road
Purney
London SW15 1AZ

Designer: David West
Editors: Gail Bushnell, Kate Newport

Photo Credits
U.S. Navy photo by Erik K. Siegel, 1; Flight International, 6bl, 6-7, 7b, 10, 13, 15,
28; U.S. Navy photo by Bryan W. Taylor, 16; U.S. Navy photo by Todd Reeves, 20;
TRH pictures, 22, 23; U.S. Navy photo, 29

1 2 3 4 5 6 10 09 08 07 06 05

TABLE OF CONTENTS

THE HARRIER JUMP JET

The AV-8B Harrier is the only U.S. fighter plane that does not need a runway. It does not even need an aircraft carrier.

The Harrier takes off and lands vertically, just like a helicopter. The U.S. Marines use the Harrier to support forces on the ground. The Harrier attacks enemy troops and helicopters. It can also defend itself against enemy aircraft.

The AV-8B Harrier is a VTOL aircraft. VTOL stands for Vertical Takeoff and Landing. Helicopters also take off and land vertically. The Harrier is much faster than a helicopter.

HISTORY

After World War II (1939–1945), planes with jet engines began to take over the skies. Aircraft designers experimented with jet planes that could take off and land vertically.

THE FLYING BEDSTEAD

In 1954, the British flew the first jet that could take off vertically and hover like a helicopter. The strange-looking aircraft was given the nickname the Flying Bedstead. It proved that an aircraft could take off vertically and land again on jet power alone.

THE SHORT SC1

The Short SC1 was a research aircraft first flown in 1957. It used four jet engines to take off vertically. It also had a fifth jet engine to make it move forward. The system worked, but it was very complicated.

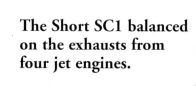

The Short SC1 balanced on the exhausts from four jet engines.

The Flying Bedstead hovered on the exhaust from two jet engines.

THE HAWKER P.1127

The Hawker P.1127 was the first jet that could take off vertically, fly around, and then land vertically. The Hawker P.1127 flew for the first time in 1960. It took several years to turn this research aircraft into a useful combat aircraft. The first British Harrier squadron started flying in 1969.

The U.S. Marines first became interested in the Harrier in 1968.

CROSS-SECTION

Take a look inside this U.S. version of the AV-8B Harrier. The labels show which pages will help you to find out more.

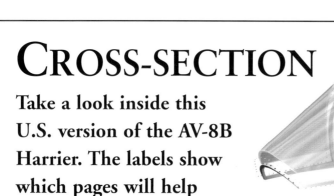

The Harrier has been built in many versions for different air forces. The AV-8B was developed in the United States from the first British Harriers. Today, the AV-8B is built by the Boeing Company.

EJECTION SEAT
See pages 18–19

COCKPIT
See pages 16–17

RADAR ELECTRONICS
See pages 24–25

AV-8B HARRIER
Wingspan: 30 feet, 4 inches (9.2 meters)
Length: 46 feet, 4 inches (14.1 meters)
Height: 11 feet, 7 inches (3.6 meters)
Maximum speed: 662 miles (1,065 kilometers) per hour
Maximum weapons load: 10,800 pounds (4,900 kilograms)

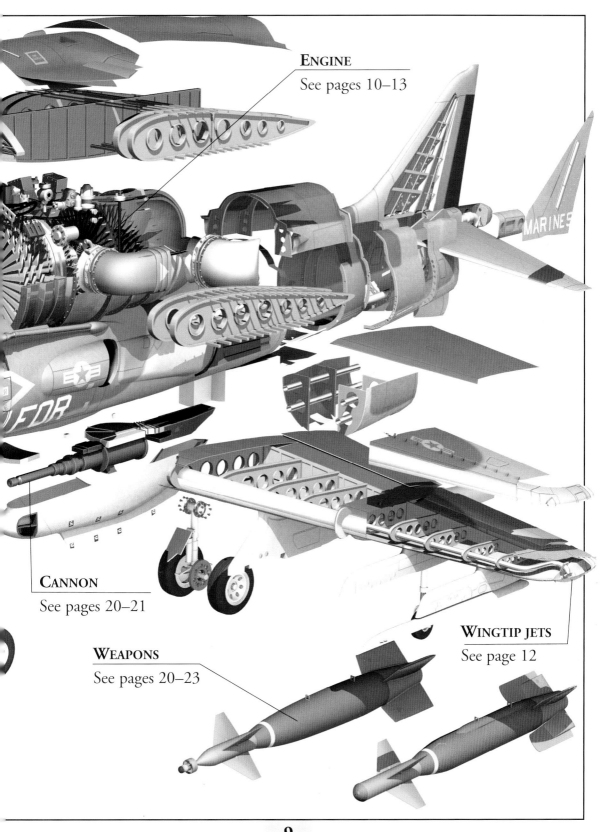

ENGINE

See pages 10–13

MARINES

FDR

CANNON

See pages 20–21

WINGTIP JETS

See page 12

WEAPONS

See pages 20–23

THE ENGINE

Most jet engines have just one exhaust. The Harrier engine has four.

In a jet engine, air is sucked in through the air intake at the front. The air is then compressed, or squeezed. In the core of the engine, fuel is burned in the combustion chamber to heat the air. The hot air expands and is pushed out through the exhaust.

This Harrier engine has been removed for inspection. The intake and exhausts are covered so dirt and mice cannot get in.

COMPRESSOR

The compressor blades turn at high speeds and compress the air.

AIR INTAKE

Air is sucked in by large fans at the front of the engine.

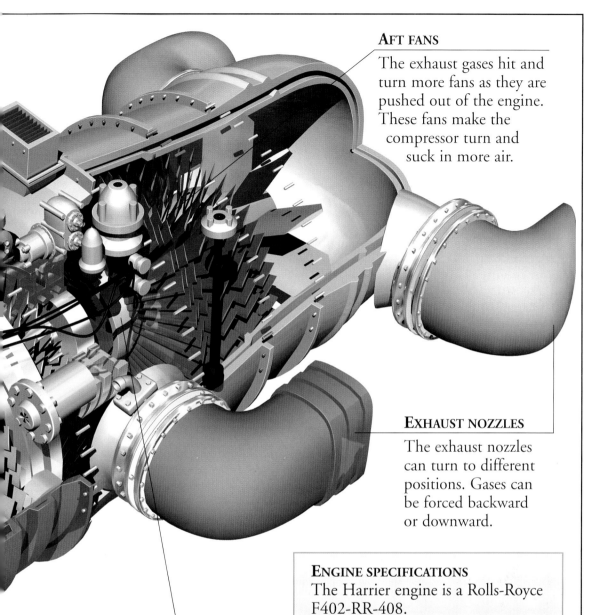

AFT FANS

The exhaust gases hit and turn more fans as they are pushed out of the engine. These fans make the compressor turn and suck in more air.

EXHAUST NOZZLES

The exhaust nozzles can turn to different positions. Gases can be forced backward or downward.

ENGINE SPECIFICATIONS

The Harrier engine is a Rolls-Royce F402-RR-408.

Thrust: 23,800 lbs (10,800 kilograms)
Normal takeoff weight: 22,950 pounds (10,410 kilograms)

The thrust from the engine is greater than the aircraft's weight, so the Harrier can take off vertically.

COMBUSTION CHAMBER

Fuel is burned here with the compressed air.

Position of jet engine in Harrier

VTOL (Vertical Takeoff and Landing)

The Harrier turns its four exhaust nozzles downward to use the power of the engine to take off vertically.

Planes use their wings to create lift. The engine provides the power to move forward. Air then streams past the wings creating lift. But the Harrier can take off using just the power from the jet exhaust.

The Harrier moves forward a short distance at takeoff. This helps the wings create lift so the Harrier can take off with a heavier load of weapons or fuel.

WINGTIP JETS
Jets of air from the wingtips help to balance the Harrier while it is taking off or landing vertically.

1. NOZZLE ANGLE 90°
Exhausts point straight down for takeoff.

3. NOZZLE ANGLE 0°

Exhausts point straight back, like on other jets. The Harrier flies forward.

2. NOZZLE ANGLE 45°

Exhausts are turned slowly backward to help the aircraft move forward.

British Sea Harriers used a ski jump ramp when taking off from Royal Navy ships.

Maneuvering

FLYING BACKWARD

The Harrier can maneuver like no other jet by balancing on its exhausts.

FLYING BACKWARD

The exhaust nozzles are pointed slightly forward to push the Harrier slowly backward. Flying backward is useful when landing the Harrier vertically in a small area.

FLYING SIDEWAYS

FLYING SIDEWAYS

By tilting the Harrier slightly, it can be flown slowly sideways. This movement helps the pilot land the aircraft in tight spaces.

THE CURTSEY

THE CURTSEY

Harriers often perform at air shows. When a Harrier finishes its performance, it hovers and lowers its nose as a curtsey to the crowd. No other combat jet can maneuver this way.

Their maneuvers make Harriers very popular air show performers.

THE COCKPIT

The cockpit is the pilot's office. It is packed with handles, instruments, and displays.

KEY TO DIAGRAM
1. Control column
2. Throttle
3. Nozzle angle lever
4. Pilot's seat
5. Ejection seat handle
6. Head-up display (HUD)
7. Computer keyboard
8. Computer screen
9. Canopy

A Harrier pilot uses the control column and rudder pedals to fly the aircraft. The throttle controls the engine. During vertical takeoff and landing, the nozzle angle lever moves the exhaust nozzles. Computers help the pilot find and hit the target. On the head-up display (HUD), the pilot can see vital information, such as speed and altitude, without looking down at the instrument panel.

The canopy on the Harrier gives the pilot a good all-around view. This view is important for vertical takeoff and landing.

16

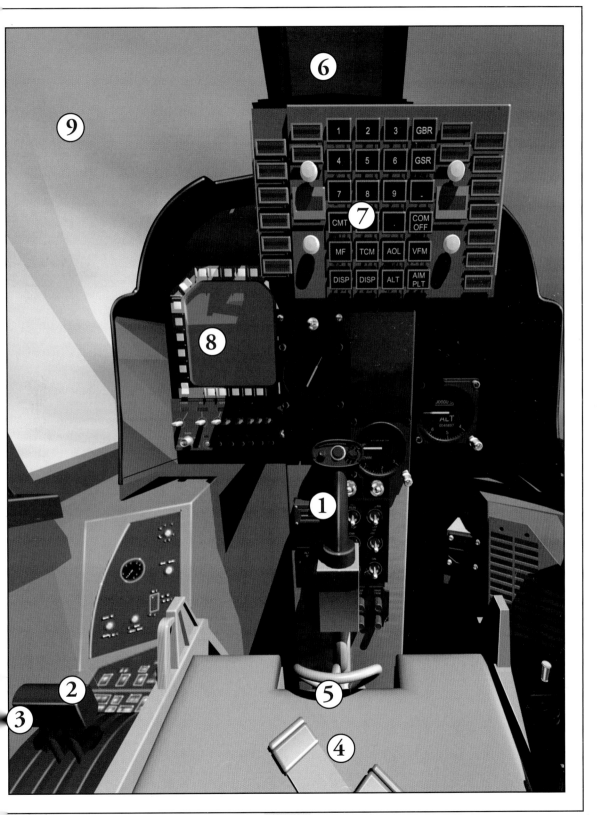

EJECT!

If an AV-8B Harrier becomes seriously damaged, the pilot needs to escape. At high speeds, this can only be done using an ejection seat.

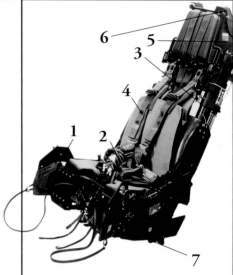

The ejection seat is designed to work both in the air and at ground level. The seat works very quickly. Just three seconds after the pilot pulls the firing handle, the main parachute opens.

Ejection is a brutal way to leave the aircraft. The pilot's body is thrown upward with incredible force. But using the ejection seat is still far better than crashing with the aircraft.

KEY
1. Leg straps
2. Firing handle
3. Guide rails
4. Harness
5. Parachute container
6. Canopy breaker (used if the explosive charge does not shatter the canopy)
7. Rocket pack

1. The pilot pulls the firing handle. An explosive charge shatters the cockpit canopy. Leg straps and harness tighten.

2. An ejection gun fires the seat up the guide rails to clear the aircraft. Then the rocket pack fires the seat upward.

The rockets under the ejection seat fire for just one-fifth of a second. The force is powerful enough to push the seat 330 feet (100 meters) away from the aircraft.

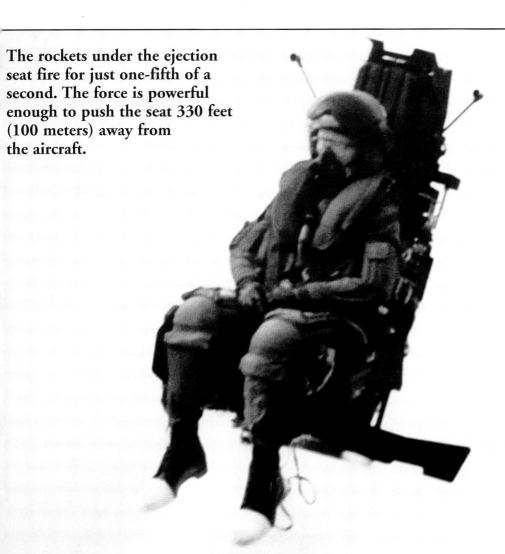

3. An explosive charge opens a small parachute. This slows down the seat and pulls out the main parachute.

4. When the main parachute opens, the ejection seat releases the pilot. The pilot then floats to safety.

WEAPONS OF WAR

The Harrier can carry different weapons to attack targets on the ground and in the air.

The Harrier is used mainly as a ground attack aircraft. It attacks targets on the surface, from tanks and troops on land, to enemy ships at sea. Harriers carry air-to-ground missiles that can punch holes in the armor of most tanks and armored vehicles. Cluster bombs spread many smaller bombs over a wide area. The Harrier can also defend itself against enemy aircraft with its air-to-air missiles and cannons.

1

2

3

4

The Harrier can be loaded with different weapons depending on its mission.

LARGER WING

The AV-8B has a larger wing than the first versions of the Harrier. The new wing is also lighter and stronger, so the Harrier can carry more weapons. A plane would not carry all these weapons at the same time.

4

7

4

4

5

6

KEY TO WEAPONS

1. AIM-120 AMRAAM
(air-to-air missile)
2. AGM-65 Maverick
(air-to-ground missile)

3. AGM-114 Hellfire
(air-to-ground missile)
4. Paveway laser guided
bomb

5. CBU-87 cluster bomb
6. Cannon
7. JDAM satellite guided
bomb

MISSILES

Harriers carry a range of missiles. Missiles can be used to attack ground targets or to fight enemy aircraft.

Most of the Harrier's targets, on the ground or in the air, are long-distance ones. Pilots often fire a missile and then go straight to another target.

All missiles use guidance systems to find their targets. Some missiles are heat-seekers. They aim for the infrared signal given off by heat. Other missiles are radar-controlled. They send out radio waves that bounce back off the target object, showing its exact location. Some missiles even have a television guidance system.

In combat, a pilot always tries to fire his missiles before the enemy even knows he has been spotted.

A British Harrier fires a number of small rockets from four launch pods.

Guidance system

Explosives

TV seeker

AGM-65 MAVERICK
This air-to-ground missile uses television guidance to find a target.

Rocket motor

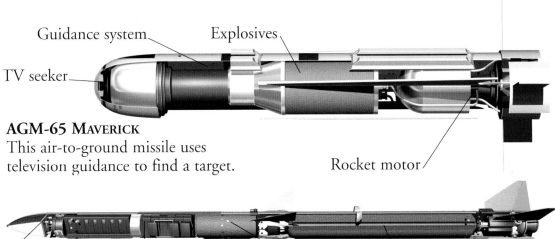

Radar antenna

Guidance system

Explosives

Rocket motor

AIM-120 AMRAAM
The AIM-120 is a radar-controlled, air-to-air missile. It can shoot down the enemy at long range without the pilot needing to have the enemy in sight.

DEFENSE

Enemy missiles are the biggest threat to the Harrier. The pilot uses electronic warnings, chaff, and flares to avoid being hit by enemy fire.

The Harrier's radar warning receivers let the pilot know if an enemy radar has found the aircraft. This means the pilot can be alert and ready to fight off the attacker.

The Harrier also sends out signals to friendly radar so it will not be mistaken for an enemy aircraft. These friendly messages are sent out by the IFF (Identification Friend or Foe) aerial.

A hot, glowing flare is fired from a Harrier. Flares are used as a defense against heat-seeking missiles

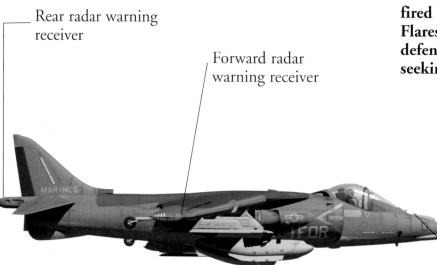

Rear radar warning receiver

Forward radar warning receiver

IFF aerial

CHAFF

Chaff are thin strips of metal foil that are shot out behind the aircraft. It confuses a radar-controlled missile so it does not hit the Harrier.

FLARES

Flares burn at a very high temperature. The heat-seeking missile aims for the hot flares rather than the exhaust from the Harrier's engine.

Chaff

Flares

Radar-controlled missile

Heat-seeking missile

THE MISSION

The Harrier is used mainly as a ground attack aircraft. What follows is a description of a typical mission. It shows how some of the Harrier's tactics and weapons are used.

Two Marine Harriers are sent to attack an enemy ground target. On their way back to base, they meet some enemy aircraft.

5. The Harriers pick up the enemy aircraft on their radar. They fire AMRAAM missiles to force the enemy aircraft away from the ships.

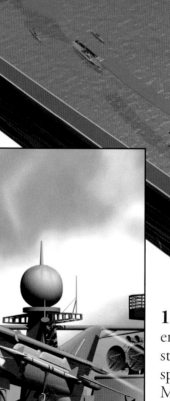

1. An enemy radar station has been spotted. Two AV-8B Marine Harriers are sent out from a ship.

4. The Harriers fly away. They fire flares to avoid being hit by any hand-held heat-seeking missiles. Then they get a message. Enemy aircraft are approaching the ships.

4

3

2

3. The Harriers destroy the enemy radar station and vehicles with Maverick missiles.

2. The Harriers fly in low to avoid enemy radar.

DEVELOPMENT AND FUTURE

The AV-8B Harrier will remain in service with the U.S. Marines for many years to come.

The Harrier has been in service with the U.S. Marines since the 1980s. It has been updated many times with better electronics and new weapons. Today, the Harrier has equipment that helps it to hit targets at night and in all kinds of weather. In recent years, the AV-8B Harrier has been involved in many missions over Afghanistan, Bosnia, Kosovo, and Iraq.

Different versions of the Harrier have been in service in Great Britain with the Royal Air Force and the Royal Navy. Harriers have also served with the navies of Italy, Spain, and India. These Harriers (*below*) are from the navy of Thailand.

Eventually, the AV-8B Harrier will be replaced by the U.S. Marine version of the F-35 Joint Strike Fighter (*inset*). This version of the F-35 will be able to hover and land vertically just like the Harrier.

GLOSSARY

aircraft carrier (AIR-kraft KA-ree-ur)—a warship with a flight deck where aircraft take off and land

canopy (KAN-uh-pee)—the cover over an airplane cockpit

chaff (CHAF)—strips of metal foil released into the air to confuse a radar-controlled missile

exhaust (eg-ZAWST)—heated air leaving a jet engine

flare (FLAIR)—a sudden burst of light and flames; Harriers fire flares to confuse heat-seeking missiles.

infrared (in-fruh-RED)—able to find objects by picking up traces of heat

mission (MIH-shuhn)—a task given to a person or group

radar (RAY-dar)—equipment that uses radio waves to find or guide objects

squadron (SKWAHD-ruhn)—a group of aircraft that go on a mission together

thrust (THRUHST)—the force that pushes an aircraft forward

READ MORE

Beyer, Julie. *Jet Fighter. The Harrier AV-8B.* High-Tech Military Weapons. New York: Children's Press, 2000.

Schaefer, A. R. *Jet Fighter Planes.* Wild Rides! Mankato, Minn.: Capstone Press, 2005.

Sweetman, Bill. *Jump Jets: The AV-8B Harriers.* War Planes. Mankato, Minn.: Capstone Press, 2002.

INTERNET SITES

FactHound offers a safe, fun way to find Internet sites related to this book. All of the sites on FactHound have been researched by our staff.

Here's how:
1. Visit *www.facthound.com*
2. Type in this special code **0736852549** for age-appropriate sites. Or enter a search word related to this book for a more general search.
3. Click on the **Fetch It** button.

FactHound will fetch the best sites for you!

INDEX